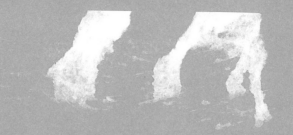

DIG, PLANT, AND GROW!

Louise Spilsbury

Heinemann
LIBRARY

www.heinemannlibrary.co.uk
Visit our website to find out more
information about Heinemann
Library books.

To order:
☎ Phone +44 (0) 1865 888066
▤ Fax +44 (0) 1865 314091
▣ Visit www.heinemannlibrary.co.uk

Edited by Harriet Milles and Adam Miller
Designed by Philippa Jenkins and Artistix
Original illustrations © Capstone Global Library
    Limited 2008
Illustrated by KJA Artists
Picture research by Elizabeth Alexander and
    Maria Joannou
Production by Victoria Fitzgerald
Originated by Heinemann Library
Printed and bound in China by South China
    Printing Company Ltd.

ISBN 978 0 431112 67 1
13 12 11 10 09
10 9 8 7 6 5 4 3 2 1

**British Library Cataloguing in Publication
Data**
Spilsbury, Louise
    Dig, plant, grow! - (Life skills)
    1. Gardening - Juvenile literature
    I. Title
    635
A full catalogue record for this book is available
from the British Library.

Acknowledgements

We would like to thank the following for
permission to reproduce photographs:
© Alamy pp. **29** (Blend Images/John Lund/Marc
Romanelli), **32** (John Swithinbank), **36** (Nigel
Cattlin); © Capstone Global Library pp. **31, 33,
45**; © Corbis/Moodboard p. **38**; © Fotolia p.
41; © GAP Photos pp. **30** (FhF Greenmedia),
26 (Marcus Harpur), **12** (Mark Bolton), **24**
(Rice/Buckland), **19** (Sharon Pearson); © Getty
Images (Stone/Mark Douet) p. **15**; © iStockphoto
pp. **42, 44** (Karen Massier); © PA
Photo/Bernat Armangue pp. **6–7**; © Photolibrary
pp. **35** (Garden Picture Library/Janet Seaton),
11 (Oxford Scientific Films); © Shutterstock pp.
40, 49 (archana bhartia), **43** (Arturo Limon), **48,
49** (Egidijus Skiparis), **47** (gemphotography),
45 (Hannamariah), **48** (Iain Frazer), **46** (Isakov
Eduard Olegovich), **46** (Jill Lang), **48** (jirijura),
48 (Kati Molin), **49** (Kheng Guan Toh), **47**
(malle), **47** (matka Wariatka), **47** (Mirec),
46 (Paul Maguire), **9** (Poznukhov Yuriy), **47**
(Rosetta-hidek), **46** (sad), **47** (Sally Wallis), **49**
(Sergey Lavrentev), **47** (Ulrike Hammerich), **21**
(Walter Pall); © TopFoto/Jim West/ImageWorks
p. **5**.

Cover photograph of boy with potted plants
reproduced with permission of © Punchstock/
PhotoAlto.

We would like to thank Dr. Kenneth R.
Robertson for his invaluable help in the
preparation of this book.

Every effort has been made to contact copyright
holders of material reproduced in this book.
Any omissions will be rectified in subsequent
printings if notice is given to the publishers.

Contents

Some words are printed in bold, **like this**. You can find out what they mean by looking in the glossary.

WHY GROW YOUR OWN?

Why grow your own flowers, herbs, or vegetables when you can make a short trip to a shop and buy all these things without any of the hassle or wait? For a start it's hard to beat the simple pleasure of watching a tiny dry seed grow as if by magic into an edible or beautiful plant, but there are many other great reasons to dig, plant, and grow your own.

IT MAKES YOU HAPPY

Gardening is relaxing, creative, and fun and it is incredibly satisfying to see your plants grow. Being outside gardening, or simply taking time to sit back and enjoy the colours, sounds, and smells of the plants that you grow helps to reduces stress levels and really can make you feel happier – just try it!

Growing plants also brightens up your house and the whole neighbourhood, which cheers everyone up. Plants attract wildlife so you can also enjoy watching the animals, insects, and birds in your garden. Scented flowers not only bring colour to the garden or windowsill, they also fill the air with perfume, which is known to enhance people's moods.

It keeps you fit

While you are gardening you are also getting exercise and fresh air. Gardening is a great form of exercise because it involves a number of different kinds of movements, including stretching, bending, and weightlifting. So various parts of the body get a work-out. It is also good exercise for your heart and lungs – and the fitter your heart and lungs, the fitter you are.

Some garden chores can be a bit tiresome, like weeding or cutting the lawn, but it helps to think of it as productive exercise – after all, a long walk or a jog won't give you a bowl of strawberries or a pot full of flowers at the end of it!

TIP

Walking briskly can burn off up to 200 calories in half an hour, which is about the same as half an hour of digging and shovelling or lawn mowing (with a hand mower).

It saves you money

There are some start-up costs to consider when you begin growing your own because you may have to buy pots and tools as well as seeds and plants. However, in the long-run growing your own saves you money. This is especially true if you like to buy **organic** vegetables (grown without the use of artificial **insecticides** and **fertilizers**). These are usually more expensive in shops than non-organic vegetables. When you grow a plentiful supply of flowers you can not only enjoy watching them grow outside but also cut some and bring them inside to cheer up your room. If you grow enough, you may be able to sell some of them or give bunches as gifts. Small plants grown from seeds or **cuttings**, or bunches of flowers, also make good items to sell for charity fundraising events or sales.

Community gardening is fun and rewarding – and brightening a dreary area with colourful flowers and shrubs can boost a whole neighbourhood.

Big issues

There are also bigger issues that persuade some people to try growing their own. One of these is "food miles". Food miles are the distance that food travels from the farm to our shops. Much of the food (and flowers) we buy in supermarkets comes from countries far away. For example, Kenya's flower industry is the biggest exporter of roses and carnations in the world.

However, people are becoming increasingly concerned about the issue of food miles because of environmental concerns. Long trips by ship and by plane generate greenhouse gases that contribute to **climate change** and also use up the world's dwindling oil resources.

In some cases, food miles are unavoidable. **Tropical** fruits such as pineapples and bananas can only be grown on a commercial scale in tropical countries. People elsewhere must import these if they want to eat them. But it is also true that many types of imported fruit and vegetables could be grown and supplied locally, or by people growing their own. By growing plants suited to our local environment we can reduce energy use, since these plants do not require extra inputs of heat or artificial light, or excessive amounts of water.

Water waste

Water is one of the biggest environmental issues in the world today. In some places the agriculture industry is draining valuable water resources, often because a country is growing crops unsuited to its climate.

For example, almost 50 litres of water are needed to produce just one 50-gram bag of salad leaves – and that does not include the water used to wash, process, and pack the leaves. In some areas of the world this is causing rivers and ponds to dry up, depriving some communities and a variety of animals the water they need for survival.

No one is suggesting that you can save the planet just by growing your own vegetables. However it is easy to grow plants like salad leaves, and by doing so you not only get a supply of fresh and delicious leaves when you want them but you save water, too.

> Once you have gardening skills **TIP** you can also rent them out! Some summer jobs are dull or tedious, such as peeling potatoes in a café or cleaning hotel rooms, but if you know your way around a garden, friends and neighbours may pay you to cut their lawns, look after their plants, or dig their gardens. You could even put up an advert in a local shop or print a card and pass it out to your parents' friends to let them know what you can do.

The flower-growing industry in Kenya is being blamed for falling water levels in the Rift Valley Lakes. There are fears that the lakes could disappear altogether from overuse.

Grow your own for variety

Growing your own food and flowering plants also gives you much more choice. Have you ever eaten a Pink Fir Apple potato or a purple carrot? If your family mainly buys its food from supermarkets the answer to this question is probably no, because these shops sell a limited range of food choices and flower types. Supermarkets usually only stock the most popular varieties, the ones that keep well and come in more uniform sizes so they are easier to stack on shelves. When you grow your own you can try the more unusual varieties, some of which also taste and look much more interesting.

Fresh is best

Flowers and foods are better fresh. Freshly picked food tastes better and if you do pick a few of the flowers that you grow, freshly picked flowers last longer. Fresh food is also more nutritious. Foods start to lose **nutrients**, such as vitamins and **antioxidants**, which help protect the body from certain diseases, as soon as they are picked. This is particularly true in the case of green vegetables such as lettuce and green beans.

Instead of buying fresh fruit and vegetables at a shop and leaving them in the fridge for a week, when you grow your own you pick and eat food on the same day, getting the maximum nutrients.

Grow your own to know your own

People also grow their own so they know what is in their food or what has been used on their flowers. Some intensive farming methods use large amounts of chemical fertilizers, insecticides, and **herbicides** (weedkillers). Not only can some of these, when used in large quantities,

When you grow your own food you naturally eat with **TIP** the seasons, because you eat what grows naturally in your country or region in the different times of the year. In addition, seasonal food tends to be fresher, tastier, and more nutritious. Eating seasonal food also means you eat a wide range of foods, making a balanced diet easier to achieve and linking with your body's natural demands. For example, in a **temperate climate**, people eat more hearty food in winter such as **root vegetables** for filling, slow-release energy. In summer people grow and eat lighter meals of salads for fast-release energy.

harm the environment, trace amounts can also linger in the food. By growing your own you will know what is on your food, and even if you do not choose to grow organically, at least you can control the amounts of chemicals you use on your plants.

*It is a fact that many foods eaten immediately after they have been picked from the plant taste better. For example, the sugar in peas starts to convert to **starch** the moment they are picked, which is why they taste so much sweeter straight from the plant.*

Plant Know-how

It doesn't matter whether you've got a big back garden, a balcony, a windowsill, or something in between, you can easily grow your own plants. But before putting your spade into the ground or buying your first packet of seeds let's get back to basics. Recapping on your plant knowledge will help a lot when it comes to thinking about what plants need.

HOW PLANTS GROW

Most plants begin life as a seed. Inside a seed there is an embryo – a tiny "baby" plant consisting of a root, a **shoot**, and two tiny leaves – and a food store. The food store keeps the embryo alive until the seed is ready to **germinate** and the tiny plant inside can start to grow. Seeds have a tough outer coat that is usually hard and dry. This is why seeds can be kept in packets or in dark conditions for months or even years, until you are ready to plant them.

Germination

Most seeds need three things to germinate: water, air, and warmth. In a temperate climate with cold winters and warm summers, seeds dropped by a flowering plant in late summer will stay in the ground until the following spring. This is vital because it means that a young plant does not try to grow just as the weather is turning cold enough to kill it.

When conditions are right, the seed soaks up water and the root and shoot inside the seed start to swell. As these get bigger, they crack the seed's coat and force their way out into the soil.

TIP

When a seed starts to grow, the first leaf-like structures to emerge are in fact **seed leaves.** These might look like real leaves, but they cannot **photosynthesize.** Only when the plant's first **true leaves** form can a seedling begin to make its own food. This is why you should never plant out seedlings until at least one pair of true leaves has grown.

The shoot from a seed grows naturally upwards towards the light. The roots grow downwards and anchor the plant into the soil.

Getting it **Right**

Knowing what plants need is useful when growing your own. There is no point planting seeds for most outdoor plants in winter, because although you might be able to germinate the seeds in a warm spot, the young plants or **seedlings** will die when planted outside. It is also useful to know why seeds need to be kept dark and dry until you are ready to plant them, and that you need to water them to help them germinate.

"Annuals" and "perennials"

Annuals and **perennials** are terms you will see a lot on seed packets or on plants that you buy. Annual plants grow from seed, flower, and then die, all in one year or growing season. Perennial plants can live for three or more years and most produce flowers every year. Many perennial plants also grow wider in diameter each year. Many perennial plants lose their leaves or even all their above-ground parts, including stems and leaves, during the winter or in dry seasons.

Properly stored seeds will only start to grow when they are planted in damp, warm soil.

Getting it Right

Soil is a mixture of air, water, **inorganic** material such as tiny pieces of weathered rock, and organic matter such as decomposed plant and animal material. When roots take in water, they also take in minerals from the rock fragments and nutrients from the organic matter dissolved in the water. These help plants grow to be strong and healthy. When you grow plants, you need to make sure you have good, rich soil to ensure your plants grow well (see page 26 for more on **fertile** soil).

"The love of gardening is a seed that once sown never dies, but grows to the enduring happiness that the love of gardening gives."

Gertrude Jekyll (1843–1932) Influential British gardener and landscape designer.

Why plants need light

Most of us know that putting a plant in a dark cupboard is likely to kill it off, but do you know why? The reason is that when the seed's food store runs out once the seed has germinated, the plant has to make its own food. It does this by using a process called photosynthesis, which basically means "putting together with light". Plants need to be able to trap light in their leaves and use that light energy to combine water and carbon dioxide (a gas in the air) to make food in the form of sugars.

Plants take in water through their roots, which is why we mainly water our plants by pouring the water on the soil at their base, near the roots. As the water travels up through a plant to the leaves it also fills out the stem to hold the leaves up to the light.

Carbon dioxide enters a plant through tiny holes on the underside of a leaf, called stomata. It is useful to remember this when caring for house plants. If they get too dusty the dust can block the stomata and reduce the amount of food that the plant can make, so dusting plant leaves or wiping large leaves with a damp cloth is really worth the effort!

names to know

As well as the basics about plant growth, it is important to know some of the basic plant terms you'll see around. Two of the most basic are **evergreen** and **deciduous**.

Deciduous plants are those that drop their leaves in autumn and look bare in winter, until they grow new leaves in spring. They do this because their leaves could be damaged by harsh weather. Some people grow deciduous plants, such as Japanese maple, especially for the lovely red, gold, yellow, and bronze colours that their leaves turn as they start to die in the autumn.

Evergreen plants, as their name suggests, are plants that have leaves that are tough enough to last all year round. They do lose old leaves throughout the year, but they do not drop all their leaves at once. Most gardeners try to plant a mix of deciduous and evergreen plants so their garden does not look completely bare over winter.

Some plants are neither one thing nor the other. Some of these semi-evergreen plants drop their leaves in especially cold winters but might keep them if the winter is mild. Other plants, such as hornbeams that are often used as hedges, have leaves that die but stay on the plant until the following spring.

Bulbs and more

When you go to a garden centre to choose a plant you can buy plants in pots, plants in seed form or, at certain times of the year, an array of gnarled, dry-looking parts called confusing names like **bulbs**, **corms**, **tubers**, and **rhizomes**. These are basically underground parts of deciduous plants that will grow in spring or summer if planted in soil.

Getting it Right

Bulbs and some other underground parts act as food stores so that plants can convert some of the sugars made by photosynthesis into starches that they can store. The plant can turn the starch back into sugar when it needs more energy – for example when a deciduous plant is ready to grow again. With bulbs, remember to let the leaves remain on the plants until they turn brown because the leaves must make an energy store so the bulb is ready to grow again next season.

Daffodils, tulips, and bluebells are types of bulbs, and bulbs are a sort of underground stem. Some plants, including dahlias and potatoes, grow from tubers. Tubers are swollen stems that act as food stores for the plant. Rhizomes are a type of stem that grows horizontally underground and produces roots. Irises and canna lilies grow from rhizomes. Crocuses and freesias grow from corms, which are swollen, underground stem bases.

Potatoes and carrots are underground food stores for plants, which is also what makes them nutritious for people to eat.

WHAT TO GROW AND WHERE TO GROW IT

You can grow a variety of plants – fruit, vegetable, flowers, and trees – in a variety of places. Whether you have a large back garden or just a windowsill or balcony, you can grow a wide range of plants for food and pleasure.

WHERE TO GROW

If you don't have a garden space already, consider other plots. Even if you have a small back or front garden covered in concrete, you can still grow a variety of plants in containers or **raised beds** filled with soil (see diagram on page 17). On balconies, you can grow plants in containers on the floor, and use trellises or other supports to encourage climbing plants to grow. You can attach hanging baskets to your outside walls or sit containers on your windowsill and doorstep. Even if you have to start on a very small scale, there may be opportunities to expand what you and your family grow by renting an **allotment** garden space.

Selecting the site

If you plan to build a raised bed or have a choice where to put your potted plants, a site near the house in full sunlight will probably be the most convenient. This is close enough that you will be able to appreciate the flowers and pick any vegetables and fruit you grow, whatever the weather.

Some plants, such as leafy vegetables, can tolerate partial shade, but most (and especially fruit plants) need sunlight. Try to avoid areas shaded by other buildings, large trees, or hedges. These will block sunlight from your plants, and tree roots may penetrate far into the soil and rob crops of moisture and plant food. If your space is affected by strong winds, put your plants by a fence. This will act as a windbreak and protect your plants from the gales.

TIP

Some people worry about growing food plants near roads because they fear that fumes from car exhausts may make the food unhealthy. This used to be a problem when cars ran on leaded petrol, but today pollution from exhaust fumes can be washed off with water.

HOW TO MAKE A RAISED BED

[Ask an adult to help you with this project.] Measure your plot and make a note of the dimensions of your raised bed. Prepare the site by raking the ground to level it, and patting it smooth. Dig 4 holes at each corner, around 10–15 cm deep and approximately 15 cm diameter.

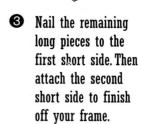

You will need:

- 8 wooden planks measuring 5 x 15 cm, cut into 4 longer lengths for the sides, and 4 shorter lengths for the ends.
- 4 posts 8 x 8 cm width, cut to 45 cm lengths. Use cedar wood, or another weather resistant wood. Sharpen one end of each post.
- 32 spiral nails 9 cm long.

TRY THIS

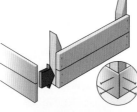

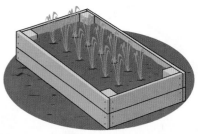

❶ On a flat surface, lay two of the shorter lengths of plank on top of two of the sharpened corner pieces. Nail the planks to the corner pieces.

❷ Stand one short side on its end and nail the end of one of the longer planks to the outside of the corner post.

❸ Nail the remaining long pieces to the first short side. Then attach the second short side to finish off your frame.

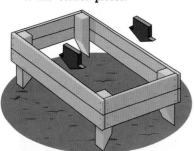

❹ Flip the frame over and lower each pointed corner post into the holes you have dug. Push down until the frame is "flush" with the ground.

❺ Fill the frame with soil, and smooth it over with a rake. Dampen the soil with a hose. Your bed is ready to plant up!

17

Container planting

You can keep pots or troughs of flowers and vegetables on a windowsill, sheltered balcony, or in a conservatory almost all year round. The great thing about growing plants in containers is that you can move them around. This means you can put them outside in warm weather, to brighten up a doorstep for example, but also allows you to move plants to a shadier spot if the sunlight is too strong on a windowsill. This is especially important for young seedlings that can get scorched (burned) if they are in full sunlight.

If you have a wide, sunny windowsill, you can grow things like tomatoes, peppers, cucumbers, and aubergines in regions where it is too cold to grow these vegetables outdoors.

Good drainage

Remember, unless you are growing marsh or bog plants, which need waterlogged soil to survive, your containers will need to have holes in the bottom for excess water to drain through. If your pot does not already have drainage holes, make some by forcing a skewer through the base if the pot is thin plastic or ask someone to drill holes through if it is wood. To stop the drainage holes getting blocked by soil as the soil gets compacted (squashed), fill the bottom quarter of the pot with some bits of broken pots or stones before putting any soil in it.

Another very important thing to remember is to sit pots on a waterproof tray. Many plants – and especially seedlings that can be killed by overwatering – prefer to take up water from below, rather than have their soil soaked through. A waterproof tray will also protect any surfaces from water spillage.

You can make plant containers out of all sorts of unexpected items. Here, an old rubber tyre is being used as a container for a courgette plant.

You don't have to choose to grow EITHER food OR flowering plants! If space is limited, why not try growing vegetables and flowers or other ornamental plants together? Many vegetables look attractive enough to be grown in the flowerbed among flowers. Other vegetables can be grown entirely in containers next to flowers or shrubs in pots.

TIP

RECYCLE YOUR OWN POTS

You really don't have to spend a fortune on buying fancy pots at garden centres. There are lots of different types of containers you can use, including recycled items like washed-out yoghurt pots and other food containers, old buckets, plastic storage boxes, half barrels, old dustbins, old chimney pots, and old sinks.

WHAT TO GROW?

The choice of what to grow can seem daunting at first. Start by deciding what you want from your gardening venture. Do you want to grow only food, for example, or do you want to brighten up a space with flowers and other ornamental plants? Read the checklist on pages 46–49 to help you choose which plants you would like.

Herbs

Herbs are attractive and add flavour and nutrients to a meal. Try annuals such as basil, coriander, and parsley; or perennials such as mint, rosemary, lavender, and sage; or even bulbs such as chives. You can grow herbs in a garden bed, in hanging baskets, or in pots on a windowsill or doorstep. Grow them near a door so they will be within easy reach for picking.

Fruit and vegetables

Many fruits grow on trees and take time to produce fruit, so start with fruit bushes. You could grow gooseberries or blackcurrants in the garden, blueberry plants in containers, or strawberries in pots or hanging baskets.

For balcony spaces, try climbing fruit plants such as grapes and passion fruit. Cucumbers and peppers grow well in largish pots on windowsills. Potatoes, courgettes, and carrots will grow in smallish spaces or big pots, and climbing beans and peas can be grown up a trellis. Salad leaves, such as rocket, grow very easily in a window box or pot in a sunny spot.

Ornamental plants

To create an attractive flowerbed try for a mix of flowering plants that flower in different seasons to give longer-lasting interest. Try to include some evergreen plants. These provide a backdrop to the flowers as well as some colour in winter because they have leaves all year round. Many trailing flowering plants, like nasturtium, work in hanging baskets. Climbing flowers such as clematis grow well up a trellis and many flowers, small trees, and grasses do well in pots.

Getting it Right

To preserve some of your herb crop for after the growing season is over, try freezing them. Freezing keeps the flavour fresh and also keeps in nutrients. For most herbs, chop finely, put into a washed-out margarine pot, and make sure the lid is on tightly. Herbs should keep for up to 6 months, ready to sprinkle into soups and sauces when you want.

Gardening in miniature

If you have no room to plant trees, try bonsai gardening. Bonsai is a Japanese word that means "container growing" and bonsai is a technique of growing small versions of plants. Bonsais need a fair amount of light, which makes them an ideal plant for a windowsill. Any tree or plant can be trained to be a bonsai. The idea is basically to trim branches and keep the plant small by keeping it in a small pot to restrict the growth of its roots.

There are many different types of bonsai trees and plants to choose from so do a bit of research first. It is best to buy a kit that tells you exactly what you need to do to care for the plant, such as soil type, and the amount of water and shade the tree needs. A kit will also give instructions on how to trim the tree and train it to grow along wires to form unusual shapes.

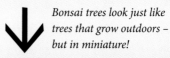

Bonsai trees look just like trees that grow outdoors – but in miniature!

MAKING A GARDEN PLAN

When you have decided what type of plants to grow, you need to plan where to put them. It helps to sit and consider how much space you have and the conditions there, for example if it is a section of the family garden. It can also help to measure the site and draw a plan of what spaces you have. Then mark on existing features in the garden, like trees, and any problem areas, such as a waterlogged patch.

When planning where to grow plants, remember that different plants have different needs. Some will thrive in sun and dry conditions, while others will prefer damp and shady locations. The reason most plants and shrubs fail to grow is that they were planted in the wrong place. When you draw a plan of your space, note where it is sunny, shady, dry, or damp to help you work out what will grow well and where.

Double up your space

In a vegetable garden you can double what you grow by grouping early crops together so that once they have finished you can fill that space with later maturing crops. For example, early peas or beans can be followed by late cabbage or carrots; early corn or potatoes can be followed by turnips or spinach. When you put different plants in one space, this creates a natural **crop rotation**.

Crops take different types of nutrients from the soil and are vulnerable to different **pests**. Planting the same crop in the same spot year after year would mean soil is robbed of a particular set of nutrients and particular pests may stay in soil and build up. Rotating crops ensures that the soil has time to recover those nutrients and pests don't have a chance to build up.

Getting it Right

Think carefully about how to fill your space so it looks good and works best. For example, plan for tall plants at the back of a border, with smaller ones in front of them to create layers of colour. Be careful to find out in advance how tall and wide each plant is likely to grow to full size, and leave enough space for it. It is very easy to get caught out by an unexpected giant that swallows up everything else. For instance, a globe artichoke can grow to over 1 m across and 1.8 m tall. In summer, the Russian vine (also known as "Mile a Minute") can grow up to 30 cm per day in all directions!

Thinking it through

Be realistic when planning your garden. Consider what you can afford, how much time you have to devote to the project, and how much to plant. It is better to have a small, well-maintained garden than a large one that is neglected and full of weeds.

This garden plan has been drawn for a 8 x 8-m area, which may be a lot larger than the space you have available. But however small your area, it pays to draw a plan so that you can make good use of every inch.

Work out a scale so that you can draw the plan onto squared paper. For example, a scale of 1:50 means for every 1 metre you need to draw 2 centimetres on your plan. Then you can decide how much seed and how many plants to buy. Finally, make sure that you leave enough room for *you*! For instance, will you be able to move easily around your planted area so that you can weed, water, **prune**, and pick?

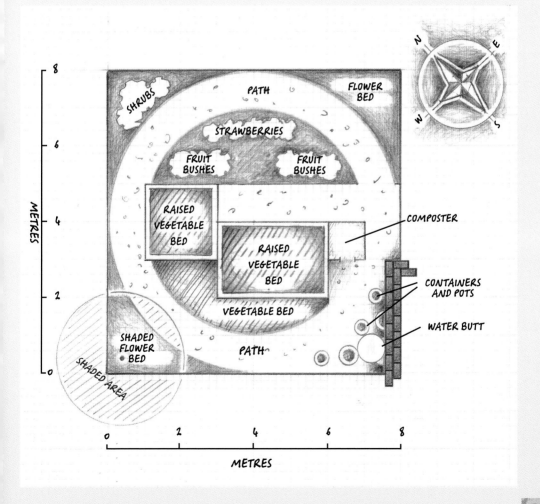

Wildlife garden

You might like to plan a themed garden, either at home or as part of a school or community project. You can create a wildlife area on any scale, from planting a few window boxes with insect-friendly flowers, to a full-scale habitat creation project with animal hiding or nesting places such as bird boxes. Remember to include maintenance in your planning and budgeting.

Pond plantings

Different plants live in different places in a pond. Some grow below the surface and add oxygen to the water, others have floating leaves that provide shade, and some grow on the margins, giving shelter for wildlife. A good wildlife pond should have gently sloping sides so that animals can get in and out of the water easily, and a range of depths to encourage a good diversity of wildlife.

MAKE A SENSORY GARDEN

You could create a sensory garden, designed to stimulate all the senses.

- **Sight:** brightly coloured plants such as sunflowers and pot marigold
- **Sound:** grasses that rustle in the breeze such as greater quaking grass or a bamboo
- **Scent:** hyacinths, lavender, chocolate cosmos, sweet peas, and honeysuckle
- **Touch:** furry-leaved Lamb's ears, silver sage and Jerusalem sage, or spiky sea holly
- **Taste:** herbs such as oregano and spearmint.

TRY THIS

You don't need many tools for a small garden. For pots you may only need a trowel (looks like a small spade) but for larger spaces you may need a spade or garden fork, a rake, a hoe, possibly a wheelbarrow, and a garden hose or watering can to water the garden. Try to buy a few good-quality tools that will last.

Getting it Right

HOW WILL YOUR GARDEN GROW?

What sort of garden would best suit your personality? Try this quiz and then turn to page 50 to find out!

1) What kind of things do you display on a shelf or desk?
a) Pine cones, pebbles, or other natural objects
b) Brightly coloured cards and ornaments
c) Flowers and framed family photos
d) It would be tidy, with a few books or small items
e) A jumble of things.

2) What is your clothing style?
a) Shorts or baggy trousers, a T-shirt, and comfy shoes
b) Bright colours
c) Floral prints or traditional shirt and trousers
d) Smart and simple
e) Whatever is in easy reach.

3) What would your dream holiday venue be?
a) Log cabin in the woods
b) Beach hut under palm trees
c) A romantic country cottage
d) Modern city penthouse
e) Plush hotel with room service.

4) What does your room look like?
a) Wholesome with lots of natural fabrics
b) Vibrant and modern with bright colours
c) Full of fabrics and florals, or traditional with wooden furniture
d) Sleek, simple, and tidy with plain colours
e) A mess — you never have time to tidy it or make your bed!

Digging and Planting

Once you have decided what to grow and where, you can get down to the business of digging or planting the area. Containers or raised beds can simply be filled with good **compost**, but if you are using existing soil you will need to dig it over and prepare it.

PREPARING THE SITE

Use a garden fork to dig and sift soil to get rid of roots of perennial weeds such as ground elder, bindweed, and Japanese knotweed. Remove these completely or they come back year after year. Most annual weeds will pull out fairly easily, or you can use a garden spade to turn the soil to bury them as this cuts out the light they need to survive. Digging also loosens soil, allowing in air that plant roots need, letting water drain through it more quickly, and making it easier for roots to grow through soil.

Soil fertility

The top layer of the soil is the most fertile part because it contains mostly organic matter, which is full of nutrients. To nourish tired soils or simply to make your soil as productive as possible it is a good idea to add plenty of compost before planting. You can buy or make your own compost (see page 27). Use a spade to dig and mix compost into the top 30 centimetres of the whole soil area, not just the spots where you will be planting. This helps provide water, air, and nutrients to plant roots.

Worms are essential for good-quality soil. Not only do they aerate the soil, but worm poo is such a good fertilizer that gardeners call it "Black Gold"!

MAKE YOUR OWN COMPOST

Compost is a decomposed mixture of
household leftovers and garden scraps.
You can buy a composter or make your own. A mesh
holding unit is the easiest and cheapest to make. It is also
easy to lift, so that you can access the finished compost at the bottom of the pile.

You will need:

- A 3 m x 1 m length of stiff fencing
  material, such as plastic mesh
  fencing, that will stand on its own.

- A few short lengths
  of heavy wire to
  use for ties.

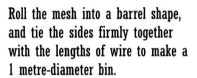

Roll the mesh into a barrel shape,
and tie the sides firmly together
with the lengths of wire to make a
1 metre-diameter bin.

You can add virtually any organic
matter to compost, except perennial
weed roots or seed-heads. You
should also avoid meat, dairy, and
cooked foods as these can attract
rats and mice. Try a mixture
of items such as raw vegetable
peelings, fallen leaves and grass
cuttings, tea bags, eggshells, waste
paper, and cardboard. It might take
a while for your pile to rot down,
but you will know it is ready
when the mixture is dark brown
and crumbly.

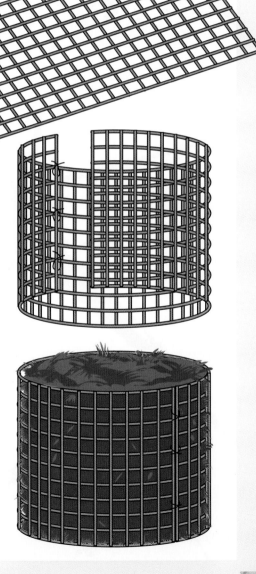

BUYING SEEDS AND PLANTS

You can buy seeds or young plants in plastic pots from garden centres, nurseries, online from websites, or from mail order catalogues (which post young plants and seeds to your home), and even from some supermarkets and corner shops. Buying seeds is cheaper and gives you a greater choice. However, buying potted plants is the best or only way to buy certain plants, which is great if you only need a few plants or don't have space to bring on seeds yourself.

Seed selection

As well as telling you the number of seeds in the packet and how many plants you should be able to raise from them, seed packets also contain information to help you choose the right plant for your garden or plot. They tell you whether the plants need shade or sunshine, moist, well-drained, or dry soil, and what height and spread the plant may reach so that you can decide whether you have room for it. Seed packets also tell you when a plant will flower and for how long, and warn you of potential pests or diseases. Seed packets should also say when to plant the seeds and how long it takes for them to germinate.

Choosing a good plant

There are several things to look out for when buying plants in pots. Flowers should match the description and picture on the label. Leaves should be a rich colour, undamaged, and with no signs of pests or diseases. Avoid pots that are full of weeds and covered with moss, or full of compost that has completely dried-out. A good test of a healthy plant is to knock on the pot gently. The compost should not move because what you are looking for is a plant that fills the pot with roots.

> **Keeping a garden diary** is a good way to record the plants you grow and how well they do. You just need a ring-binder or bound notebook with at least 12 lined pages. Write a month at the top of each page and note the year you start keeping the diary. Highlight anything special you want to remind yourself of the next year and include photos of how the plants look across the seasons.
>
> **TIP**

*When you have **transplanted** your new plant you can tuck the label into the pot or in the soil next to the plant, to remind you of the plant's name and needs. However, plant labels fade in time, so for future reference why not copy the plant's details in your garden journal (see TIP box), or even create a plant database on your computer?*

Planting seeds

Sow annual seeds in small pots or seed trays filled with compost 6 to 8 weeks before planting the seedlings in your outdoor garden. Keep them on a windowsill or in a greenhouse until the seedlings are strong enough to be planted out and there is no danger of frost. The label will have instructions for what depth to plant the seeds, and how much water they need.

Many annual seeds can be planted straight into the soil outdoors. First dig or scrape out a drill, a shallow trench where you want your plants to grow. Sprinkle smaller seeds or place larger individual seeds into position. If you are planting several or more seeds, plant in rows or mini-rows. This will help you tell the difference between seedlings and weeds when they start to grow. Check the seed packet to find out how far to space the rows apart.

TIP

To grow a new plant from a cutting, cut a side shoot or healthy stem from a parent plant. Cuttings from plants that like dry conditions should be put into coarse sand; stand cuttings from plants that like wet conditions in a glass of water; plant other cuttings in a normal well-drained potting mix. Place somewhere shady but not dark and gently spray leaves with a little water now and then until new roots form. Then put the new plant into its own pot of compost to grow it on.

Planting bulbs

Bulbs can be planted straight into pots or the ground. Most bulbs, including tulips, should be buried about three times deeper than their diameter. Groups of flowering plants look more natural if planted in odd numbered clumps, such as three, five, or seven together.

Once seedlings in a row have their true leaves they will get crowded. Pull out smaller, weaker plants to leave remaining plants more room to grow.

MAKE YOUR OWN SEED-STARTING POTS

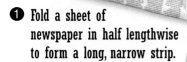

1 Fold a sheet of newspaper in half lengthwise to form a long, narrow strip.

2 Make another fold about 7 cm in from the folded edge.

fold

3 Turn it over, and place a tin can (a glass or beaker would also do) at one end, level with the folded edge, and with the closed end of the tin at the folded edge.

4 Roll the paper around the tube into a cylinder. About half of the strip of paper should overlap the open end of the tin can.

5 Push the ends of the paper into the tin to close the end. Then pull the tin out.

6 Use the closed end of the tin can to squash the folded end of your newspaper pot flat and seal the base.

7 Fill your paper pot with soil and seeds. When the seedlings grow, tear off the bottom of the pot and plant out. The pot breaks down quickly in the soil, leaving the plant roots to grow freely.

Transplanting seedlings

To transplant seedlings to the garden or to a bigger pot to allow them to establish a strong root system, gently hold the seed leaves and ease the plant and its roots out of the compost using the end of a pencil. Lift seedlings one at a time and never hold them by the stem or roots, as this could damage the plant.

Supporting the plant on the pencil, transfer your seedling to a ready-made hole in soil or compost, making sure the leaves are above the level of the compost and they are at least 4 centimetres apart.

Hardening off

Young plants that you have bought at a garden centre or seedlings you have grown yourself should be gradually **hardened off**, or made tough enough to withstand the elements, before planting in the open garden. Leave them in an open garage or on the porch during the day and then bring them in again at night, especially if there is a chance of frost or rain.

After about a week they should be hardened off enough to be planted in your garden, so long as the weather is mild enough. If it still gets chilly at night you can protect seedlings with cold frames or home-made mini greenhouses (see box opposite).

TIP

Before transplanting a well-grown plant from a pot, water the plant well about 15 minutes before planting. Dig a hole about twice the diameter and depth of the pot. Turn the plant out of its pot, stand it in the centre of the hole, and check that the best side is facing forwards and the top of the rootball is level with the surrounding soil. Fill the hole with a mix of compost and soil, firming it down gently, and water in well.

MAKE A MINI-GREENHOUSE

TRY THIS

Cut a 2-litre plastic soft drink bottle into two halves. Remove the label and the cap. Prick some holes in the bottom half for drainage. Fill with moist compost, and plant your seedlings. Cut 2–3 slits about 2 cm long downwards from the top rim of the planted half. Then push the top half of the bottle over the bottom half, so it overlaps by about 3 cm. Stand in a saucer or tray to hold water. Once your plants have grown tall enough to touch the top of the inside of the bottle, remove the bottle. Don't let the plant grow through the top or you won't be able to remove it and your plant will not thrive.

QUIZ

HOW GREEN FINGERED ARE YOU?

(Answers on page 51)

1) An annual is a:
   a) yearly check-up at the doctor's
   b) plant that lasts for years
   c) plant that lives for one season and releases seeds.

2) A flowering plant is healthy when:
   a) someone else takes care of it
   b) it buds and blooms
   c) its stem is strong, leaves are a rich green, and it grows good-sized flowers.

3) Bulbs are things you:
   a) use to light up a room
   b) should always plant in spring
   c) can plant in spring, summer, or autumn, with the bud facing up.

4) It is best to plant out seedlings:
   a) when you have a spare moment
   b) on a hot sunny morning
   c) following a spring or summer rain when soil is damp.

5) A garden drill is:
   a) a loud noise
   b) a machine to make holes
   c) a shallow trench in which to sow seeds.

CARING FOR YOUR PLANTS

Individual plant needs vary, but in general you should keep the area around your plants fairly weed-free, keep them watered during dry spells, and ensure that the soil is fertile. The amount of time you need to spend will depend on the size of garden you have and what you grow. But unless you have a very big plot you are unlikely to spend more than one hour per week on it, on average.

PLANT CARE

Some plants are pretty maintenance-free. Once you have planted them, you may need to keep watering them until they are established, but then you can sit back and enjoy them. Other plants may require more attention. For example, container plants need a lot more water than those in beds. Plants with thin stems and heavy flower heads or fruit, like tomatoes, need **staking**. This means they need to be tied to a cane or post or a metal or plastic frame to stop them collapsing. They droop because, unlike in the wild, plants in borders are often spaced apart and cannot rely on other plants for support.

Many flowers, such as roses, also require **deadheading**. This is when you cut off dead or faded blooms from a plant to prevent seed production and thereby encourage the plant to produce more and more flowers. Roses and some other plants also need pruning, or cutting back at the end of their growing season.

Pruning keeps plants, shrubs, and trees an attractive shape, stops them spreading or growing too big, and keeps them healthy by encouraging fresh, young growth. To prune, use secateurs or loppers (special garden scissors) to completely remove very thin, dead, diseased, or dying stems and any branches that are too long or spoiling the shape of the plant.

Getting it Right

Keep a record of monthly chores in your garden diary. For example, you can jot down when seedlings should be ready for transplanting, or when a row of carrots is due to be **thinned out**. You can use these reminders year after year.

Periods of dry weather are becoming increasingly common in many places, which many people believe is caused by climate change, so people are finding ways of conserving (saving) water. Garden water sprinklers can use 1,000 litres of water in an hour. Try to use a watering can instead and water plants in the early evening or morning, to reduce the amount of water lost to **evaporation** in the heat of the day.

TIP

Save water by buying a rainwater butt. These containers collect rainwater that drips off roofs into guttering so you can use it for watering plants. Rainwater is also better for your plants than tap water, which is treated with chlorine. You can also get a system to filter and reuse greywater, the waste water from washing machines and sinks.

Pest control

Pests are insects and other animals that eat or otherwise damage your plants. Some people spray with chemical insecticides and pesticides to kill small pests such as slugs, snails, and insects. Other people avoid pesticides because they may also kill helpful animals, as well as pests. For example, slug pellets harm frogs, birds, and hedgehogs – animals that are natural slug and snail predators! People may also avoid pesticides because they don't like the idea of even small traces of the chemicals being in the foods they grow.

If you have a problem with larger animal pests, such as dogs and rabbits, the only solution is to surround the garden with a fence, if there is not already one there. You can then use the fence as a trellis for supporting beans, peas, tomatoes, and other climbing crops.

Slugs and snails do not like to move across rough surfaces, so put broken eggshells, grit, or gravel around plants that are particularly at risk, such as these young hosta plants.

Here are some suggestions for natural bug deterrents:

- Plant marigolds near plants you want to protect from blackfly and greenfly. Marigolds produce a scent that deters both these insects.

- Onion plants repel mice and spider mites.

- Make your own spray of liquid soap or garlic mixed with water.

- Wind a band of copper tape (available from garden centres) around plant pots to protect against slugs and snails.

- Powdered ginger is an effective natural snail and slug repellent.

- Encourage birds to your garden and they will eat caterpillars. Put out bird seed and peanuts, and fill a shallow tray with water for the birds to drink and wash in.

Natural alternatives

There are alternative methods of pest control. Covering plants with netting prevents butterflies from laying their eggs on plants such as cabbages, so that the larvae that hatch out can eat the leaves. You can mix up your own natural insect repellents, such as several tablespoons of ground cloves with water, or try organic alternatives such as neem oil.

You can also try **companion planting**. This means growing plants that deter pests with their smell, or that attract animals that eat the pests. For instance, growing the herb coriander amongst your vegetables helps to deter aphid pests. Some people simply plant more than they need and accept they will lose some plants to the pests. Looking on the positive side, caterpillars may devour some garden plants, but they soon turn into butterflies that help pollinate others!

Weed prevention

Digging or pulling up weeds can be time-consuming, so some people resort to weedkillers. Using these poisons can be avoided if you **mulch** the area around your plants. Mulching means covering the soil with a layer of material such as wood chip, gravel, grass cuttings, bark, or black plastic. It works because mulches stop light from reaching the weeds. Without light they cannot grow, because they cannot photosynthesize. Mulching has the added advantage of keeping moisture in the soil, so reduces the amount of watering you have to do.

FEEDING YOUR PLANTS

If you dig compost in to your soil before planting, your plants may not need extra fertilizer during their growing season. However fertilizers are useful because they add nutrients to the soil and so increase crop yields and produce long-flowering plants. The best times to feed your plants are right at the beginning of the season and then regularly throughout the main growing period. There are basically two kinds of fertilizers you can buy. Organic fertilizers are made from natural substances such as plants and animals. Inorganic fertilizers are artificial, manufactured "chemical" feeds.

Getting it Right

You will need to feed container plants more often. You can buy slow-release pellets which you mix into the compost as recommended by the manufacturer, or apply a liquid feed once or twice every two weeks throughout the growing season.

Using fertilizer properly can increase the number and size of the flowers, fruit, and vegetables your plants produce.

Powders and liquids

To use granules or powdered fertilizers and feeds, sprinkle thinly over the soil. This is often called "top dressing" in gardening books. Remember that plants drink food up through their roots, so water the ground thoroughly to dissolve the fertilizer into the soil.

Liquid fertilizers are easy to apply and best for seedlings (only apply after seedlings have grown their true leaves) and potted plants. Check the labels on all fertilizers and do not overdo it. If the solution is too concentrated it will burn the roots. However if you use too little it may not be effective.

Natural alternatives

Many people make and use their own compost (see page 27) to feed the soil. Just spread a layer of compost evenly over the soil around the plants. You can also use animal manure, such as well-rotted horse dung, but never use manure from animals that eat meat because it is too acid for plants, and it smells bad. Most manure contains weed seeds so be sure to mulch your garden well so they don't get a chance to grow in your vegetable and flower gardens. You can use dead leaves or grass cuttings as mulch. Leaves contain lots of nutrients and also attract worms and **micro-organisms** that help to aerate the compost pile and speed up decomposition.

Getting it Wrong

Peat is a spongy moss that is popular with gardeners, either as a soil improver or for growing plants in. However, peat bogs are important sites for wildlife, and they are under threat from overuse in gardening. Try to use compost or other organic matter, or other peat alternatives as these can give equally good results without damaging a valuable wildlife habitat.

What fertilizers contain

The vital ingredients in organic and inorganic fertilizers are:

- Nitrogen to encourage leaf growth. Nitrogen deficiency is one reason green leaves turn yellow.

- Phosphorus to encourage root growth. It also increases a plant's ability to resist diseases.

- Potassium to encourage fruit and flower production. It also helps increase a plant's disease resistance.

Here are some ideas for things to make and cook with some of the plants that you grow.

GAZPACHO RECIPE

Gazpacho is a refreshing cold Spanish soup to eat in hot summers. You could use your own onions, cucumbers, peppers, chives, and parsley in this recipe. Serves 6–8 people.

Ingredients:
- *680 g (24 oz) ripe tomatoes*
- *1 purple onion, finely chopped*
- *1 cucumber*
- *1 sweet red or green bell pepper*
- *2 stalks celery, chopped*
- *1–2 tbsp chopped fresh parsley*
- *2 tbsp chopped fresh chives*
- *1 clove garlic, minced*
- *¼ cup red wine vinegar*
- *¼ cup olive oil*
- *2 tbsp freshly squeezed lemon juice*
- *2 teaspoons sugar*
- *Salt and fresh ground pepper to taste*
- *6 or more drops of Tabasco sauce to taste*

Method:
1. Peel and de-seed the tomatoes. To peel them, place them in boiling water for about 30 seconds, then lift them out with a spoon and the skins should come off easily. (Alternatively you can leave seeds in.)
2. Chop up the tomatoes and cucumber. Peel and chop the onion. Remove the seeds and stalk from the green pepper and chop that up, too.
3. Now put all the ingredients in the blender and blend until the soup is smooth. (You might need to do this in batches depending on the size of your blender.) Pour into a non-metal serving or storage bowl and stir in a little cold water to thin it slightly – anything from 150 to 275 ml (5 to 10 fl oz). Cover the bowl with a lid or foil and refrigerate overnight.

STRAWBERRY JAM

Jars of homemade strawberry jam make great birthday and Christmas gifts and they won't even cost you much! The recipe below should make about five jars of jam. Be careful while making this recipe that you don't get splashed with boiling jam.

Ingredients:
- *1.8 kg (4 lbs) strawberries*
- *Juice of 2 lemons*
- *1.8 kg (4 lbs) sugar*

Method:
1. Prepare the glass jars that the jam will be poured into by sterilizing them. Wash them in hot, soapy water and then rinse. Heat the oven to 175°F (80°C). Place the jars and lids open side up on a baking tray. Place in the oven for 25 minutes. Be careful and wear oven gloves when removing the hot jars from the oven.
2. Take the leaves off the strawberries and hull them (take out the tough cores). Put them in a large bowl and crush them.
3. Put the crushed strawberries into a large pan with the lemon juice and sugar. Stir over a low heat until the sugar is dissolved.
4. Bring to the boil and boil rapidly for about 10 minutes. The jam should be at setting point when the temperature reaches 220°F (105°C). To check setting point has been reached, use a sugar thermometer or try the following test: spread a teaspoon of jam on a chilled plate. When the jam is cool, touch it with your finger. The skin on the jam should wrinkle slightly.
5. Remove the scum with a flat spoon. Then leave to cool slightly.
6. Wearing protective gloves, spoon the jam into the warm, sterilized jars and seal while still warm.

PESTO RECIPE

Pesto sauce made with fresh basil is delicious stirred into pasta. Why not serve with a tomato or green salad from your garden, too? For a peppery alternative, you can also make this pesto using rocket instead of basil.

Ingredients:
- *125 g (4½ oz) basil*
- *2 garlic cloves*
- *50 g (2 oz) walnuts or pine nuts*
- *50 g (2 oz) parmesan*
- *80 ml (3 fl oz) extra virgin olive oil*
- *Salt and freshly ground pepper to taste*

Method:
1. Place the nuts in a food processor and roughly chop them. Add the basil and a little salt and pepper. Grate and add the parmesan cheese. Peel and finely chop the garlic cloves and add.
2. Switch on the processor, and blend the mixture until it is smooth, scraping down the side occasionally. While the motor is running, gradually pour in the olive oil until well mixed.
3. Spoon the pesto into a clean jar and pour a little extra olive oil over the top. Seal well with a tight-fitting lid and store in a fridge until ready to use. (It will keep for up to a month in a well-sealed jar in the refrigerator.)
4. To serve, stir a large spoonful through a bowl of cooked pasta and top with a grating of parmesan cheese.

SPANISH OMELETTE

Spanish omelette, or tortilla, is made with eggs, onions, and potatoes. It is thick and filling, and can be eaten in slices, hot, warm, or even cold for a picnic.

Ingredients:
- *5–6 small potatoes*
- *1 small onion*
- *6 eggs*
- *1 tablespoon olive oil*
- *Salt and freshly ground black pepper*

Method:
1. Scrub or peel the potatoes and slice them thinly. Peel and slice the onion.
2. Heat the oil in a pan over a medium heat and gently cook the potato slices.
3. While the potatoes are cooking, break the eggs into a bowl, add a pinch of salt (optional) and some black pepper, and mix well with a fork.
4. When the potatoes are just soft take the pan off the heat. Use an egg flip to remove the potato slices and put them in the egg mixture. Give it a stir.
5. Put the oily pan back on a medium heat. When the pan is warm, pour the egg and potato mix into it. Cook gently for 6–8 minutes or until it is turning golden brown underneath and is just ever-so-slightly liquid on top. While this is cooking, turn on the grill to medium heat.
6. Put the pan straight under the hot grill for just a minute or two until the omelette has set and is golden brown. Switch off the grill and slide the tortilla on to a plate.

Lavender retains most of its wonderful scent when dry.

MAKING DRIED FLOWERS

Drying flowers is a great way to enjoy the flowers you grow for a long time and dried flowers also make lovely gifts. Some flowers work better than others so experiment to see which ones work for you.

How to dry flowers

1. To get the best results, pick flowers in dry weather. If you pick flowers after it has been raining they may go mouldy because there is moisture trapped in the leaves and petals. Ideally cut the flowers just as they are beginning to bloom and the petals are new. Older flowers often lose their petals as they dry out.

2. Strip off all of the leaves growing from the stems as these hold water and slow the drying process.

3. Cut the flowers to a similar length. Make small bunches of the same type of flower and bind together using ribbon, twine, or raffia. Tie the string tight enough to hold the bunch together, but not so tight that it cuts into the stems.

4. Hang the flowers upside down in an unused cupboard or dark room. This should be somewhere well ventilated (airy) to help the drying process and prevent rotting. To hang the flowers use hooks, poles, or wires and space the bunches out so that air can circulate through the flowers.

5. Flowers take up to about a month to fully dry out. Once dry, carefully separate the bunches and mix flower types to create attractive arrangements. When they are done, you can spray them with a little hairspray to give them some extra protection.

POT POURRI

Pot pourri is a mixture of fragrant dried flowers and herbs that infuse rooms with a gentle scent. You can remove the petals and buds from your dried flowers to make your own. To make pot pourri you need:

- Dried flowers and herbs
- Essential oils (fragrance oils) to reinforce the natural perfumes of flowers and herbs
- Spices and herbs
- Fixative, such as orris root, to absorb and preserve the fragrance of the herbs and flowers.

ROSE DELIGHT

1 cup pink rose petals

1 cup red rose petals

½ cup small rose buds

1 cup dried lavender

1 tablespoon dried orris root

7–8 drops rose essential oil

PURPLE HAZE

1 cup dried lavender (Lavandula)

7–8 drops lavender essential oil

2 tablespoons dried orris root

½ cup pink carnation flower heads (Dianthus)

½ cup (bright yellow) lemon or orange marigold flower heads (Tagetes)

(In this recipe orris root acts as the fixative to preserve the fragrance of the herbs and flowers.)

HOW TO MAKE A POT POURRI

1. Put dried petals and flowers into a large glass or metal bowl.

2. Add the fixative, for example the powdered orris root. Add the essential oil.

3. Put the pot pourri in a paper bag and seal the top with pegs or clips. Gently turn the bag over several times to mix the ingredients. Store it away from direct sunlight for four weeks. Shake the bag gently from time to time.

4. Then place the pot pourri in an open container in a warm place. Alternatively, you can create small fabric bags and put pot pourri inside. These make clothes cupboards smell lovely if hung inside.

5. If the scent starts to fade you can perk up the pot pourri by adding a few drops of essential oil and mixing with your hands.

PLANT CHECKLIST

Here are some plants for different patches in your garden. Most are easy to grow, but before buying check the label to see that they suit your soil and your particular patch, and how big they grow. Follow label instructions for times of planting and how much to feed and water them.

Japanese Skimmia

Honeysuckle

Pulmonaria

Nasturtium

Flowers for shady places

- Evergreen shrubs such as Japanese Skimmia and Japanese barberry are happy in shade and dry soil.

- Climbing plants that cope with shade include some varieties of honeysuckles and climbing hydrangea.

- Pulmonaria or lungwort produces pink or blue flowers. Some varieties have leaves with white markings that look like paint splatters. It thrives in moist, well-drained shade.

- Flowering perennial Aconitum, or monkshood, can grow over 60 centimetres tall, prefers damp soil, and produces violet blue, or white flowers.

- Perennial geranium "Wargrave Pink" produces long-lasting pink blooms even in a shady patch.

- Bergania has large, glossy green foliage, pink flowers, and thrives in a well-drained, moist site in light shade.

- Bleeding hearts have red or pink heart-shaped flowers.

- Epimedium is good under trees where it is dry and shady. It grows to 30 centimetres in height, has heart-shaped leaves, yellow or red flowers, and crimson leaves in autumn.

- Polemonium or Jacob's Ladder grows up to 46 centimetres tall with fine, fern-like leaves that can be green or green and white and blue flowers.

- Both the peppery leaves and the red, pink, orange, or yellow flowers of nasturtiums are edible. You can sow seeds straight into the garden. Nasturtiums will grow in direct sun or shade.

Lavender

Flowers for sunny spots

There is an enormous range of flowers that thrive on full sunshine. Here are a few reliable old favourites:

- Lavender and rosemary are Mediterranean plants that can cope with spells of drought and thrive in sunshine.

- Sunflowers are easy to grow from seed or indoors and then transplant. You can get tall or dwarf sunflowers in a range of oranges and yellows.

- Phlox is a medium-height annual that comes in shades of pinks, purples, and white. It makes an attractive addition to flower beds, and lower-growing varieties can be planted in borders or edges along walkways. You can plant phlox seeds straight into the garden, but you will need to dead-head the plants to keep the flowers coming.

- Marigolds come in a range of vivid colours. Sow seeds where they will grow. They can also be sown indoors and transplanted outdoors when the danger of frost has passed.

- Common snapdragons can tolerate partial shade but do best in full sunshine.

- Cosmos is easy to grow straight from seed in the garden. The flowers are great for cutting or pressing, and attract butterflies.

Sunflower

Marigold

Cosmos

Agapanthus   *Hostas*

Acer

Plants for pots

More or less any plant can be grown in a container. Try different sized pots and different types of plants to get an interesting variety.

- Agapanthus has tall blue or white, globe-shaped flowers that grow from bulbs.

- Hostas grown in pots are easier to protect from the slugs and snails that love to eat them. Just put a layer of grit over the top of the soil to deter these pests.

- Ornamental grasses such as blue fescue and feather reed grass.

- Acers and other small trees look stunning in pots and can be used to brighten up a shady corner.

Lettuce

Runner beans

Courgette (golden)

Parsley, basil, and chives

Easy-to-grow vegetables and herbs

- Lettuces do best in full sunshine or partial shade. Sow seeds in spring in shallow rows and water regularly.

- There are many varieties of green beans, such as French, runner, and string, and most prefer full sun. Beans grow from seed in spring but you will need to provide supports as the thin stems grow by twining themselves around canes or trellises.

- Potatoes grow from seed potatoes or old potatoes that have started to chit (sprout shoots). You do need to keep them watered and to cover plant sides with soil as they grow.

- Courgettes can be easily grown from seed, either started off on a windowsill or planted straight into the garden. You need to water these regularly.

- Cherry tomatoes can be grown from seed or seedlings. They need sun so you should grow them against a wall that faces the sun and is sheltered. They can be grown in a "grow bag", but you have to make sure that they get lots of water.

- Parsley is not easy or quick to grow from seed, but you can buy cheap parsley plants. Repot the plant in a larger pot with good compost, then water and feed regularly for a constant supply.

- Chives can be grown from seed and reach around 30 cm tall. They die back in winter and re-emerge in spring. Eat the bulbs as mild onions, chop the leaves for flavouring, and add the purple flower heads to salads.

- Basil plants need sunshine so are ideal for pots as you can move them to sunny windowsills. Seeds grown in pots of potting compost will start to grow within two weeks. Water regularly at the base of the plant (they don't like water on their leaves) and pinch out (break off) flowers when they grow, to encourage more leaf growth. Cut leaves from the top of the plant when you want to eat them.

- Rosemary seeds grow slowly so most people buy small rosemary plants. Rosemary plants grow well in a sunny spot in the garden and can grow to a metre tall, or more.

- Rocket seeds can be grown in pots or outdoors. Plant a few seeds every two weeks for a long-lasting supply. Like all salad leaves, rocket needs regular watering. Snip off leaves as you need them and the plant will continue to produce more.

Easy-to-grow fruit plants

Fruit bushes or plants need a sunny area, but space is not usually a big issue as many also grow well in pots. Even if you only have room for one or two plants, you will be amazed how much fruit a little bush can produce.

- Strawberries do well in pots but good drainage is essential as strawberries will suffer in waterlogged soil. Put a layer of broken terracotta pots or stones in the bottom of the container before filling with compost and planting.

- Blueberries grow to 1.2 m and are ideal for a smaller garden or a large pot on the patio or balcony. Buy the plants bare-rooted (not in pots) and plant in early spring. They start fruiting after two years.

- Raspberry plants are bought as "canes" or stems with bare roots (not in pots). Plant in spring in a sunny sheltered spot about 35–45 cm apart. Raspberry canes need support so sink tall strong posts at each end of the row, attach sturdy wire between them, and loosely tie the raspberry canes to these as they grow.

- Blackcurrant plants are bought as canes, or stems with bare roots (not in pots) and should be planted 1 m apart. They will fruit from their second year for at least 10 years. When plants are two years old, prune out about a third of the old stems every winter.

Strawberries

Blueberries

Raspberries

Blackcurrants

HOW WILL YOUR GARDEN GROW?
For page 25

If you answered mostly As: You're in touch with nature and should go for a natural, wild garden. Plant lush green ferns and hostas in damp or shady corners or in pots, or a selection of wildflowers to create a meadow. To really get in touch with nature, plant yourself a vegetable garden so that you can pick fresh tomatoes, courgettes, and salad leaves for dinner.

If you answered mostly Bs:
Your ideal is a tropical jungle garden full of colourful and exciting plants in reds, yellows, lime greens, and pinks. Try planting tall grasses such as Stipa gigantica, Euphorbia characias with its lurid green bottle brushes, and Crocosmia "Lucifer" that has scarlet flowers. Dahlias come in many vibrant colours and flower for long periods.

If you answered mostly Cs:
You tend towards the rustic, old-fashioned charm of an English cottage garden. To achieve this look you should go for old-fashioned plants such as roses, wisteria, and delphiniums. Include flowers such as daisies, butterfly bush, hardy geraniums, coneflower, and yarrow. Include some traditional herbs such as parsley, rosemary, and lavender.

If you answered mostly Ds: You might like a clean-cut, refined look. The aim of the formal garden is to display blocks of colour framed by little hedges, and it is always tidy! You could create formal beds edged by box hedging that you can trim into shape. You should plant symmetrical blocks of coloured plants such as chives, pinks with their silvery leaves and scented flowers, irises, or statuesque alliums.

If you answered mostly Es: You need a simple, low-maintenance garden because you are either too busy or too lazy to be spending hours on your plants! No need to worry. There are lots of plants out there that will look great but require little attention after you have planted them. Avoid bedding plants, vegetables, and herbaceous perennials. Instead try a mixture of shrubs, conifers, bulbs, and grasses.

HOW GREEN FINGERED ARE YOU?
For page 33

If you answered mostly As: You are not so much green-fingered as a danger to plants! Don't despair. There is no need to give up and return to buying all your fruit, vegetables, and flowers from the shops; simply re-read the book and remember it this time!

If you answered mostly Bs: Your fingers are a light shade of green. You have some idea about caring for plants but you need to spend a bit more time brushing up on your knowledge.

If you answered mostly Cs: You definitely have green fingers, but you probably already know this. Your thriving plants and colourful plot are the envy of all your neighbours!

(20) Things To Remember

1. **Find out more.** Learn as much as you can about growing plants. There's a wealth of interesting tips and information in newspapers, library books, and websites.

2. **Consider your options.** Plan not only what you want to grow but what suits your plot, and what you can realistically afford in terms of cost and time.

3. **Plan for a garden that will** give year-round interest. Choose plants that flower or have interesting coloured foliage in different seasons.

4. **Don't be afraid to make** mistakes. If you fancy growing a plant give it a go. If it fails you haven't really lost anything. If a plant struggles in one position, you should be able to dig it up and replant it in a new place, or pot, so that it survives.

5. **Grow vegetables** amongst your flowers. This will look interesting as well as giving you fresh produce.

6. **Grow plants that** encourage wildlife. This is good for your garden, good for the environment, and good for you.

7. **When planting trees or** shrubs, think of the long-term effects. Check how big the plant will grow and how much space and attention it will need.

8. **Invest in some good** quality tools and look after them. Wipe them clean of dirt after use and keep them in a dry place.

9. **Mulch, mulch, and more** mulch! A mulch of bark chippings or thick layers of old newspaper will suppress weeds and hold in moisture. You can also use this method to clear patches of land.

10. **Keep a garden diary** to record when you did things and what worked well – or didn't!

11. **Keep your soil in good** condition. Fertile soil is the most important ingredient for successful growing. Remember to rotate crops in a vegetable garden, add compost to all garden beds, and feed your potted plants.

12. **Start a compost pile.** This is the cheapest way to condition your soil. It's environmentally friendly because it can reduce by up to half the amount of waste your household sends to landfill sites!

13. **Be creative.** Even if you only have space for potted plants, search jumble sales and charity shops for pots of different sizes, shapes, and colours to create an interesting display.

14. **Grow herbs and salad** leaves. These are some of the easiest and most satisfying food plants you can grow.

15. **Plant crops that you** cannot store, such as lettuce, a little but often, to avoid waste.

16. **Buy a water butt.** It's the best way to ensure you will have enough water in times of shortage.

17. **Don't overdo the** digging! Keep your back straight and take rests. Also make sure you wear sun screen and a hat while you're outside.

18. **Try to use natural** methods of weed and pest control. If some methods don't succeed, don't give up – make the effort to find alternatives.

19. **Swap or share seeds,** cuttings, and plants with friends.

20. **Relax!** The idea is not to have a perfect garden but to take time to enjoy the sights, scents, and sounds your hard work has created!

Further Information

BOOKS

First-time Gardener, Kim Wilde (Collins, 2008)

Gardening Basics for Dummies, Steven A. Frowine (John Wiley & Sons, 2007)

How to Make Your Garden Grow: A Beginners Guide to Popular Garden Plants, Toby and Lisa Buckland (Cassell Illustrated, 2004)

Little Book of Gardening Tips, David Curnock (Green Umbrella Publishing, 2008)

The First-time Gardener: Everything the Beginner Needs to Know to Create, Maintain and Enjoy a Garden, Jonathan Edwards (Carroll & Brown Publishers Limited, 2003)

WEBSITES

http://www.pbs.org/wnet/nature/secretgarden/
Find out how most gardens are teeming with wildlife and how to make your own garden a wildlife haven.

www.bbc.co.uk/gardening
This BBC website is a useful source for a wide range of gardening information.

www.doctorgreenfingers.co.uk
A gardening website that is clearly set out to make it easy to find the information you are looking for.

http://www.urbanext.uiuc.edu/firstgarden
A site with lots of tips for the first-time gardener.

www.gardenlings.co.uk and
www.gardeningdata.co.uk/vegetables/vegetables.php
Two sites full of useful information and links for anyone interested in growing vegetables.

http://www.farmgarden.org.uk
Find out more about community gardening and farming in urban areas.

ORGANIZATIONS

The Royal Horticultural Society
www.rhs.org.uk
The UK's best-known gardening charity, dedicated to teaching and promoting good gardening practices. The RHS runs a host of national schemes, including a new Campaign for School Gardening to encourage all schools to get out there and get growing! Check out their website to find out more.

The Soil Association
http://www.whyorganic.org
An internationally recognised authority on the principles and practice of organic gardening and farming. Visit the "Grow Your Own" section on their website for month-by-month advice and tips on successful organic vegetable growing.

National Society of Allotments and Leisure Gardeners Limited
http://www.nsalg.org.uk/
This non-profit making organization supports and advises people on all aspects of allotment gardening. As well as practical advice about successful planting and growing, the NSALG offers a discounted seed scheme and a quarterly magazine for its members.

GLOSSARY

allotment small area of land let out by councils or independent associations to people who want to grow their own food

annual plant that grows from seed, flowers, produces new seeds, and dies all in one season

antioxidant substance that protects the body's cells from damage and disease

bulb underground plant part that stores food. A true bulb has fleshy scales surrounding a central bud, but the term bulb is often used to mean rhizomes and tubers, too.

climate change change in the long-term weather patterns of Earth that is causing more extreme weather in some places

companion planting growing plants that deter pests with their smell or attract animals that eat the pests next to other plants

compost mixture of decaying organic matter, such as decomposing leaves and kitchen waste, which is used for enriching soil

corm swollen underground stem grown by some plants

crop rotation planting different crops on the same area of land to improve soil fertility and help control insects and diseases

cutting piece of a plant, such as a leaf or stem, which can be used to produce a new plant

deadheading cutting off dead or faded blooms from a plant to prevent seed production thereby encouraging the plant to produce more and more flowers

deciduous plants that lose all their leaves in winter

evaporation when water turns from a liquid into a gas (water vapour)

evergreen plants that are covered in leaves all year round

fertile soil that is full of nutrients for growing healthy plants

fertilizer substance that provides plants with one or more of the nutrients that help them grow

germinate when a seed starts to grow

hardened off process of getting a young plant or seedling that has been raised indoors used to living outdoors

herbicide chemical used to kill plants such as weeds

inorganic substance, such as a fertilizer, that has not been made or obtained from a source that is or has been alive

insecticide substance used to kill insects

micro-organism tiny living thing you can only see by looking at it under a microscope

mulch putting a layer of material, such as wood chippings, bark, or gravel, around plants to suppress weeds and retain moisture in the soil

nutrients chemicals that nourish living things, such as plants, and help them to grow

organic something that is or has been a living thing. When used to describe a method of farming, organic means grown without the use of artificial insecticides and fertilizers.

perennial plant that grows from seeds or cuttings and will survive year after year

pests living things, such as insects, weeds, mice, and others, that cause damage or are otherwise troublesome or harmful

photosynthesis process by which plants use light to combine carbon dioxide and water in their cells to make food in the form of sugars

prune to cut back plants to restrict size, train to shape, promote the growth of flower buds, or to remove dead or damaged wood

raised bed area of soil for growing plants that has been raised above ground level

rhizome stem that grows horizontally underground and that can produce roots and shoots

root vegetable vegetable that is actually the root of the plant, such as a carrot or parsnip

seed leaves leaves that are part of the tiny embryo (baby) plant present in a seed

seedling young plant grown from a seed

shoot part of a plant that grows upwards out of a seed, towards the light

staking tie to a strong stick or post for support

starch type of carbohydrate, a type of food that supplies living things with energy, which is stored in plants and used for food

temperate region of the world that has warm summers and cold winters

thinning out removal of some plants, or parts of plants, to make room for the growth of others

transplant to grow a seedling or plant indoors and then plant it outdoors, or to dig up a seedling or plant from one place and then plant it somewhere else

tropical from the tropics, the countries around the Equator, which are very hot and wet all year round

"true" leaves leaves that are produced after seed germination and that can photosynthesize

tuber short, thick underground stem that stores food and grows a new plant after winter

Index